Ukulele Picking Tunes

BEAUTIFUL AMERICAN BALLADS

by Ondřej Šárek

Oak Soprano Ukulele OA-S cover image courtesy of Lanikai Ukuleles.

WWW.MELBAY.COM

Preface

As the ukulele can be such a lyrical instrument, I have always loved hearing ballads performed on it. This book presents 25 lyrical North American melodies by known and unknown composers, scored for ukulele solo. Some of the pieces are derived from popular colonial themes, while others come from the turbulent Civil War era and up to the present day.

No collection of American ballads would be complete without settings of the exquisite melodies penned by Stephen Foster, evidenced here by *Beautiful Dreamer, I Dream of Jeanie with the Light Brown Hair* and *Hard Times, Come Again No More*—a lesser known but deserving song that seems to be making a comeback. Although written in 1854 in response to desperate pre-Civil War conditions, it is still strikingly easy for modern listeners to identify with Foster's music and lyrics.

Additional 19th and 20th century parlor or *heart* songs by George F. Root, George R. Poulton, Joseph P. Webster, Ethelbert Nevin, Edward MacDowell, and Carrie Jacobs Bond, plus a half-dozen clearly modern but stylistically similar compositions by Mel Bay Publications president, William A. Bay —round out the collection.

Using the standard re-entrant uke tuning gCEA, the arrangements in this book were written in standard notation and tablature. As an aid to the beginning ukulele enthusiast, fingering suggestions were added where appropriate. The high G or 4th string poses some interesting notation challenges, but between the two stave systems, I hope the intended 2-part musical effect is apparent.

So, pick up your ukulele, sit back, and have fun playing these timeless and new melodies!

Best wishes,
Ondřej Šárek

Contents

Just Before the Battle, Mother

Civil War Song
by George F. Root

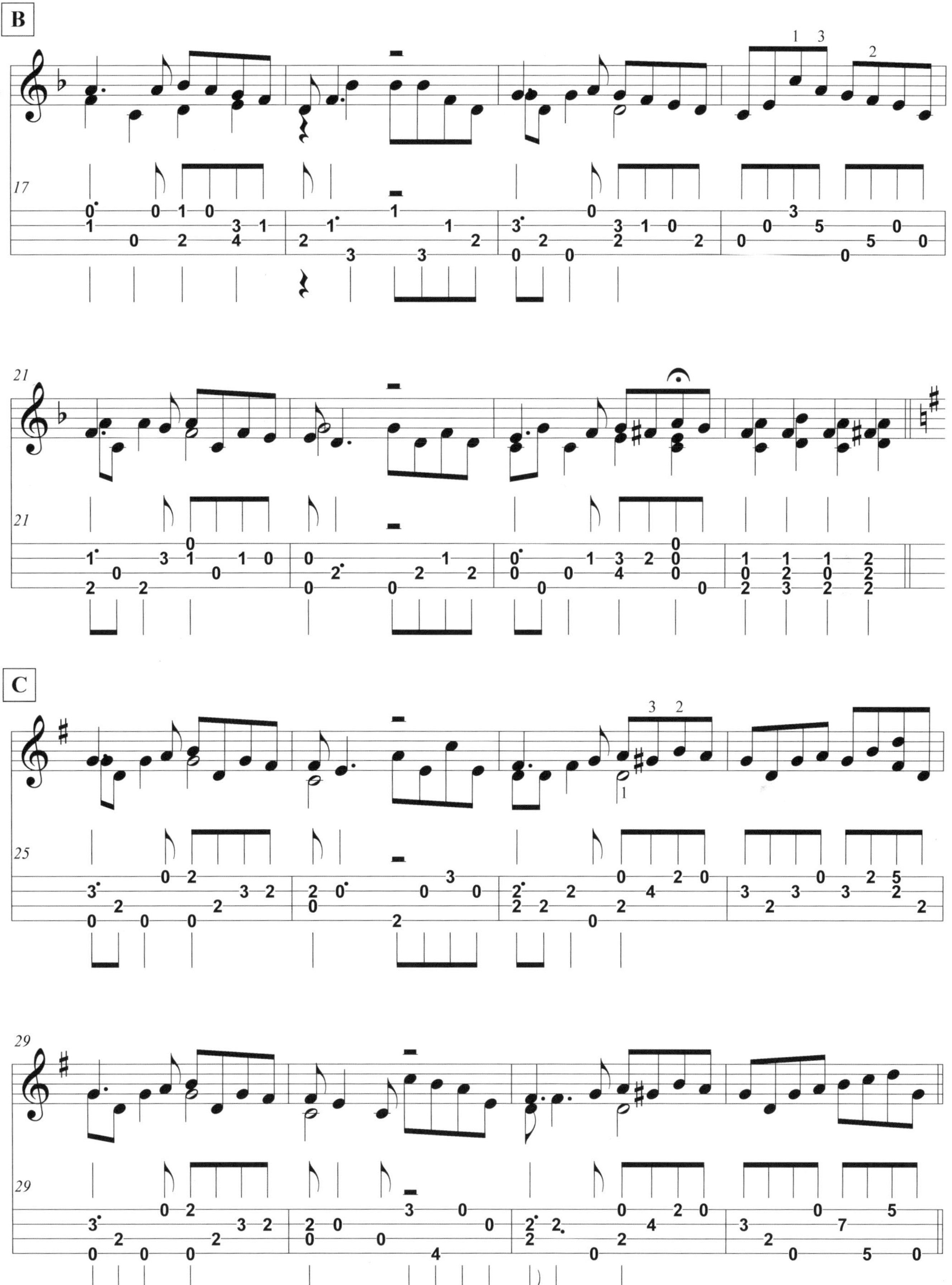
B
17
21
C
25
29

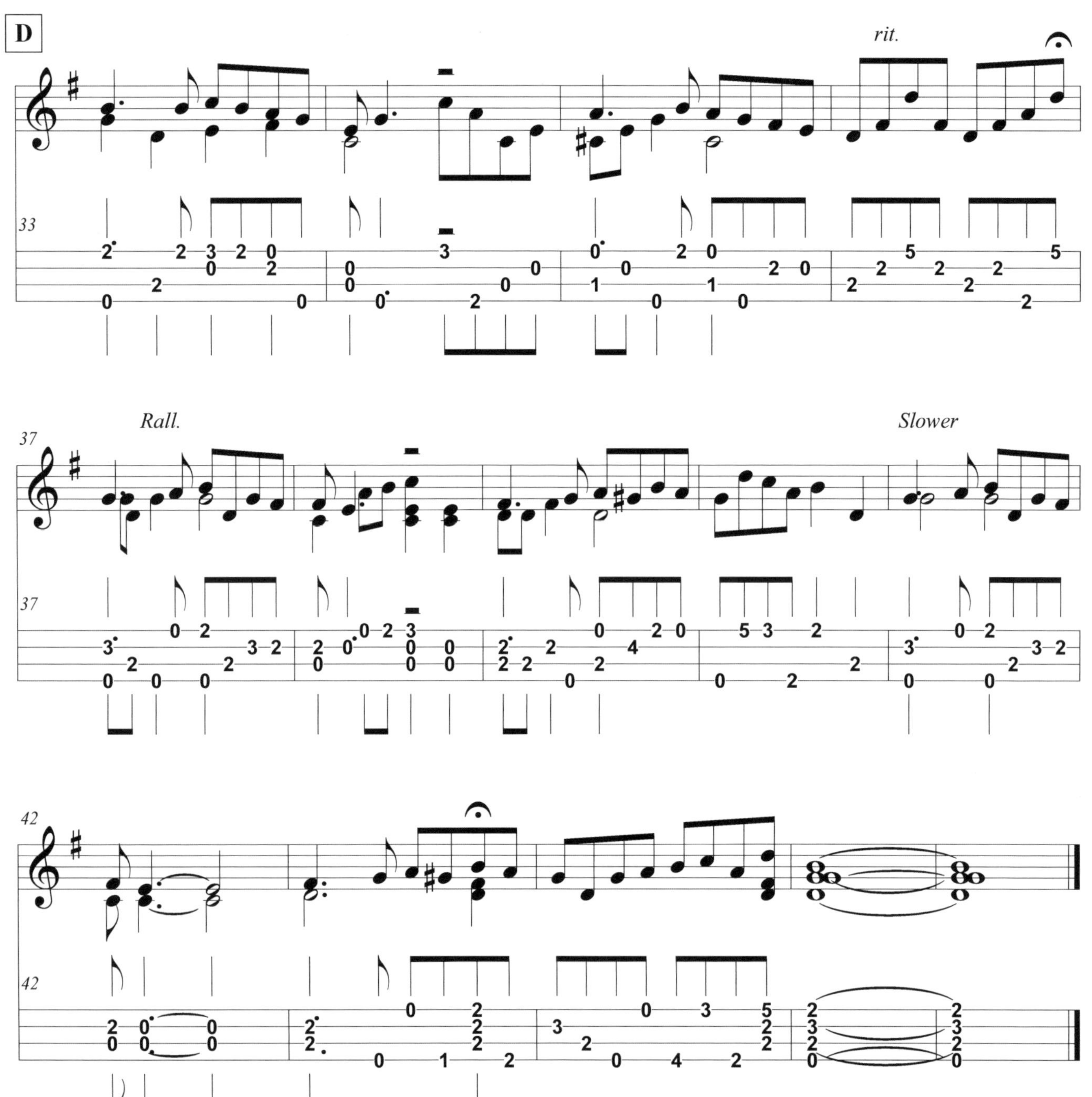
D
rit.
33
37
Rall.
Slower
42

This page has been left blank to avoid an awkward page turn.

The Old Country

William Bay

C
D.C. al Fine

The Old Homestead

William Bay

C

Aura Lee

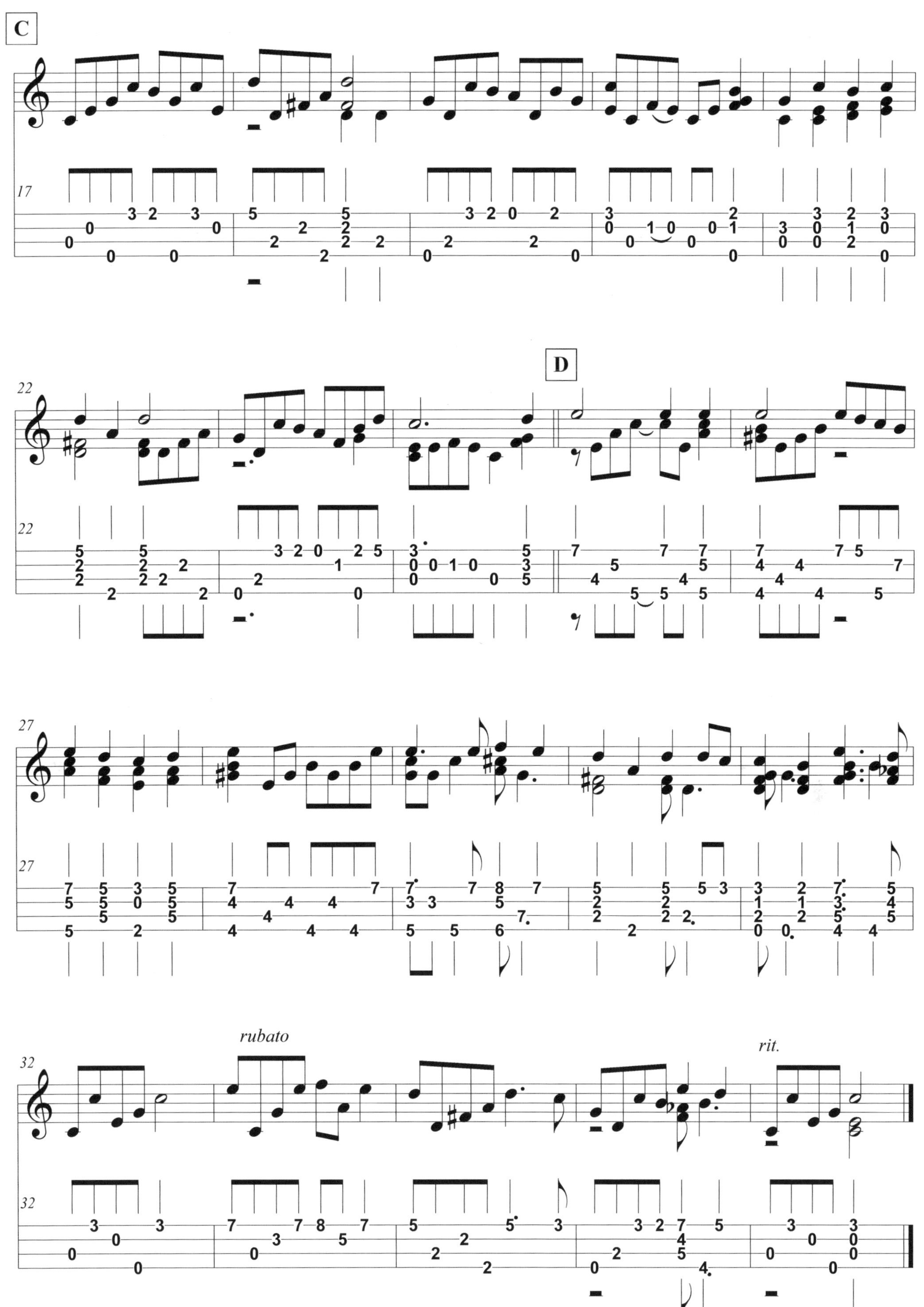
C
17
22
D
27
32
rubato
rit.

Black Is the Color of My True Love's Hair

23

28

C *With Movement*

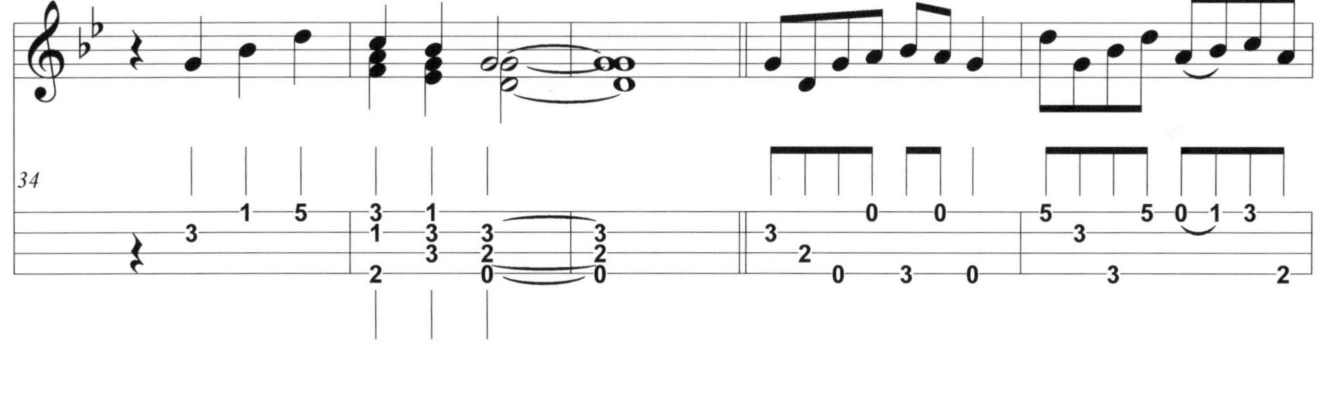

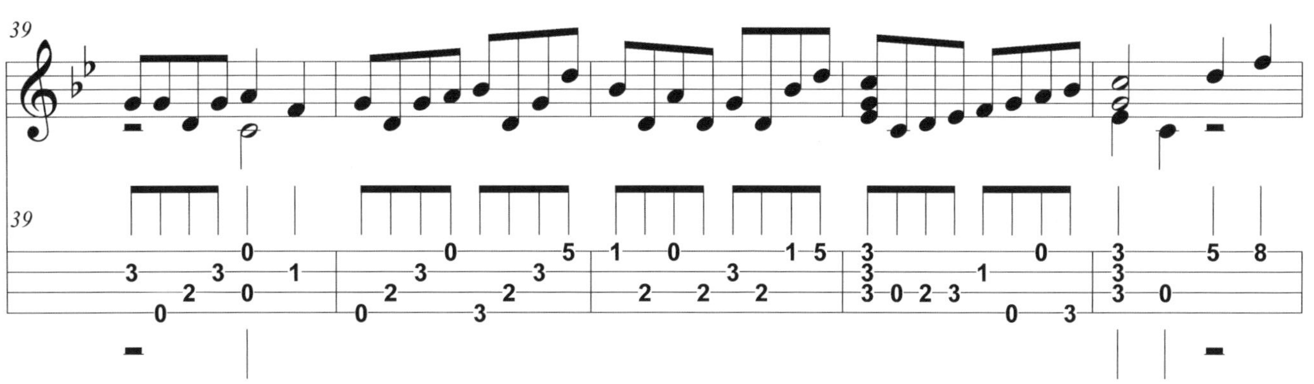

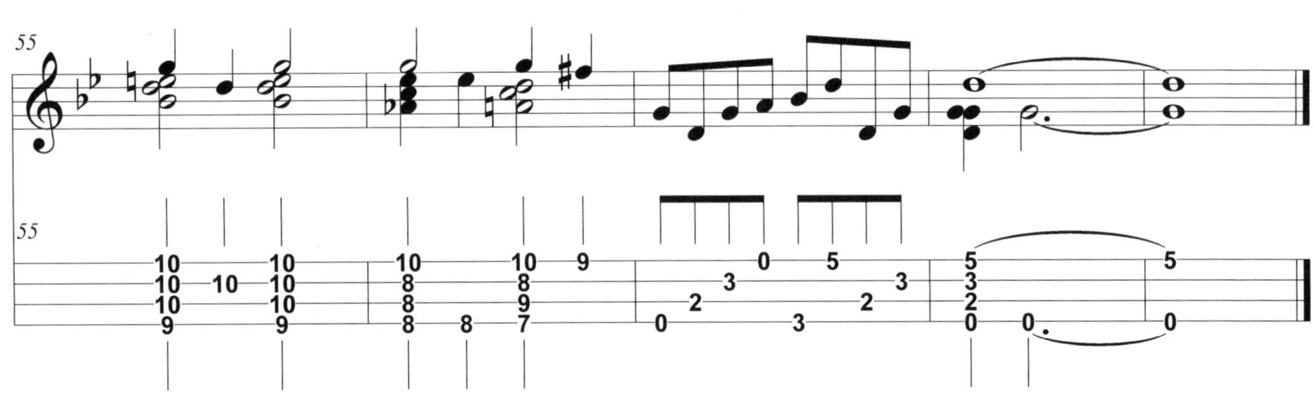

Paper of Pins

Darling Nellie Gray

Stephen Foster

C
17
17
21
21
25
25

The Long Road

William Bay

C
a tempo
17
21
rit.
D
25
29

In the Pines

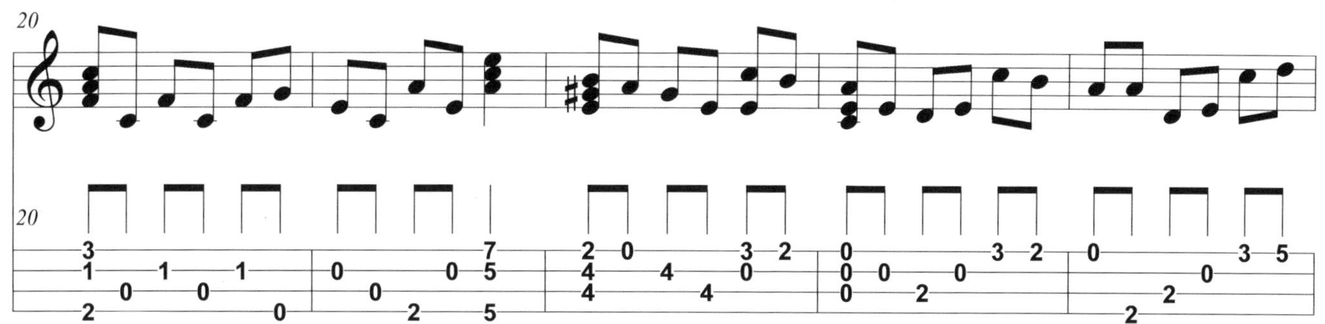

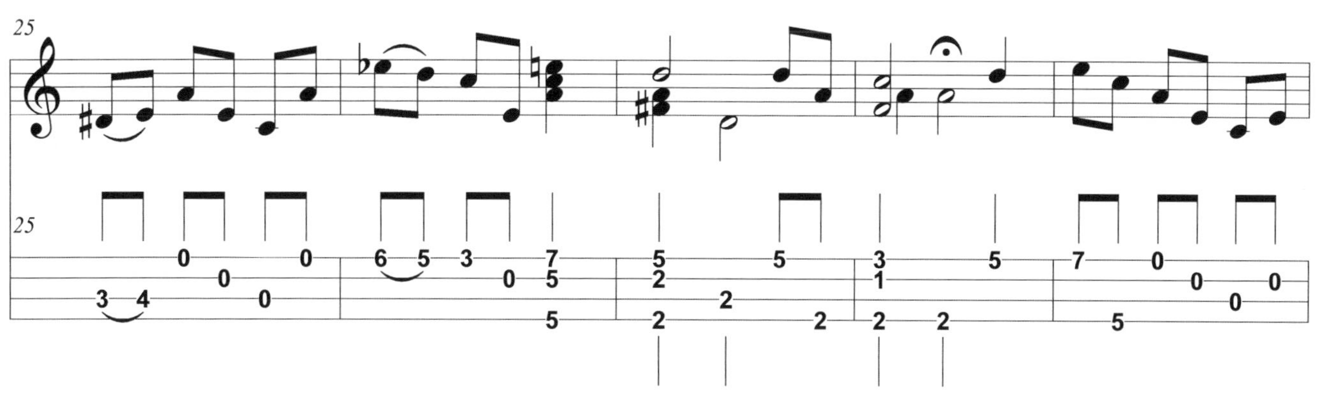

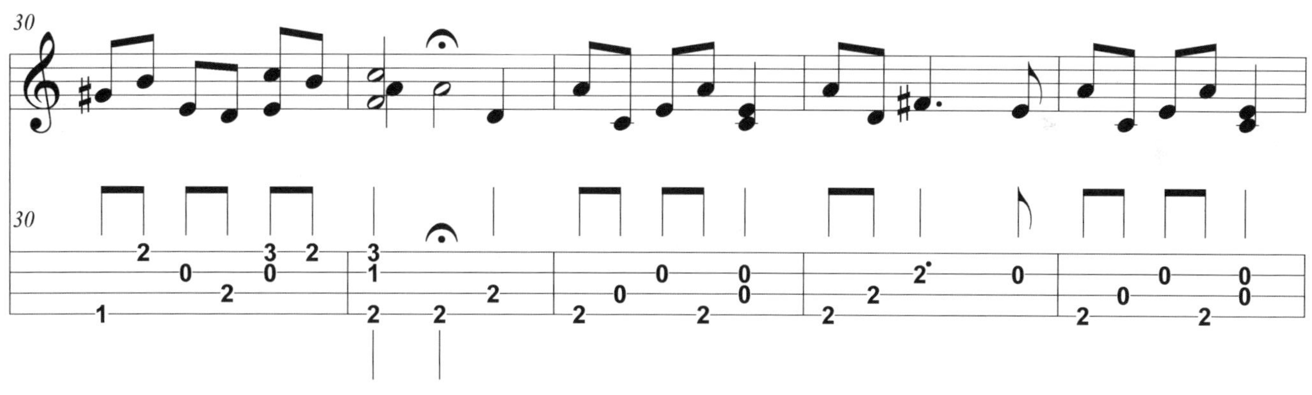

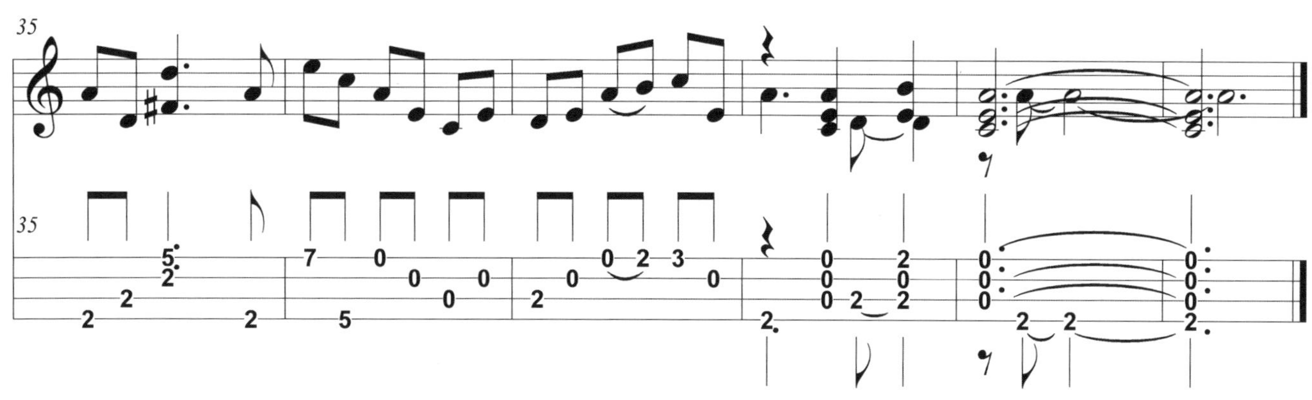

Land of Rest

Flowing ♩ = 116
Early American Sacred Melody
A
Ukulele
Ukulele
B

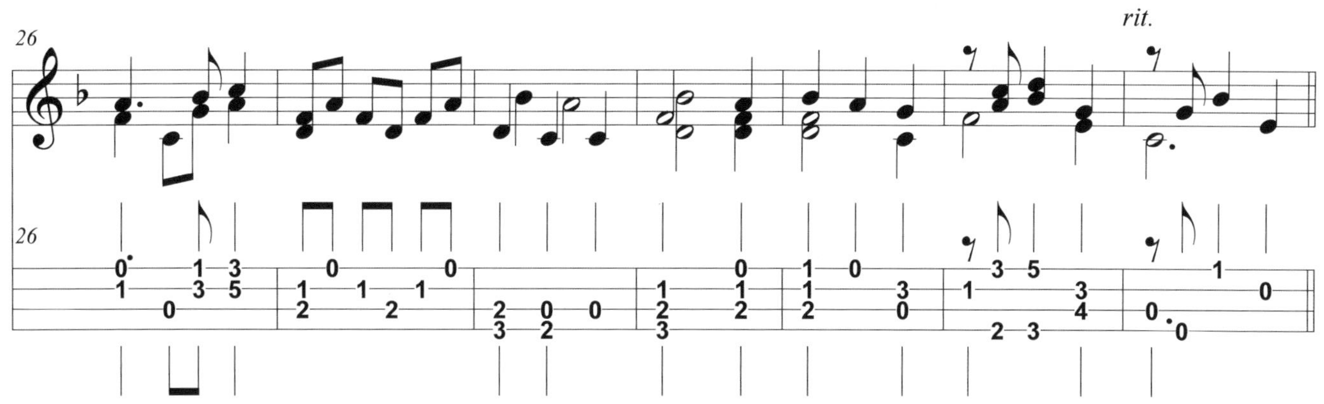
rit.

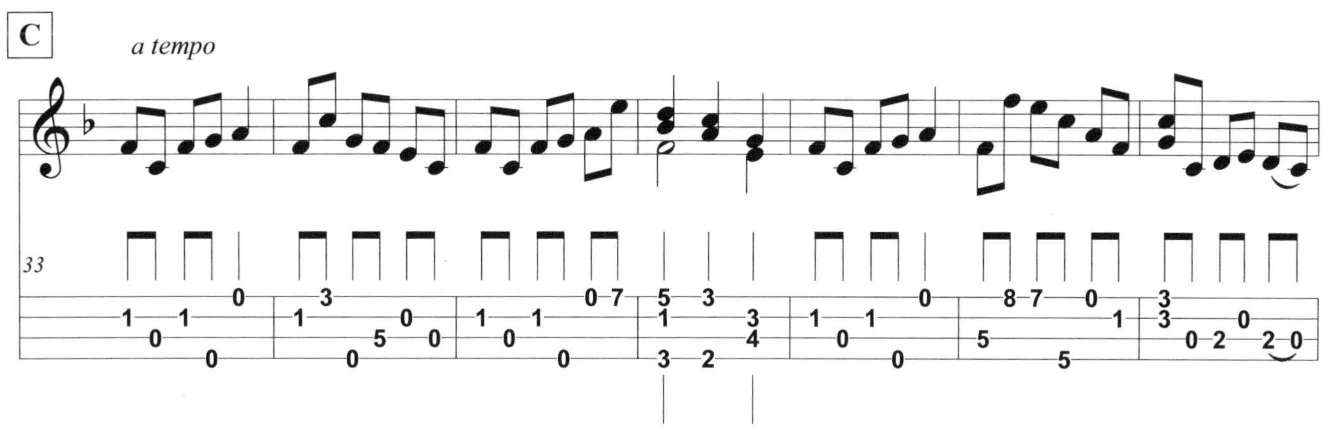
C
a tempo

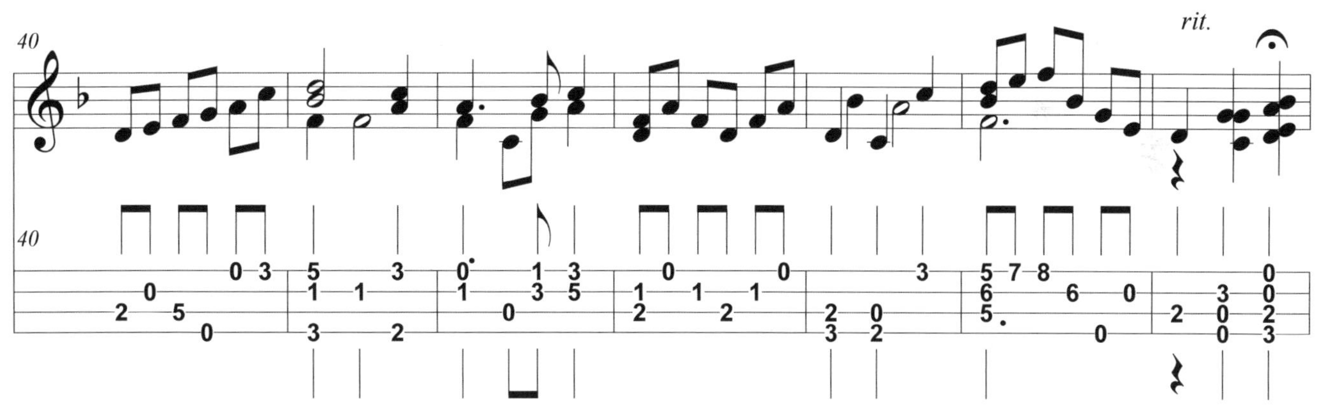
rit.

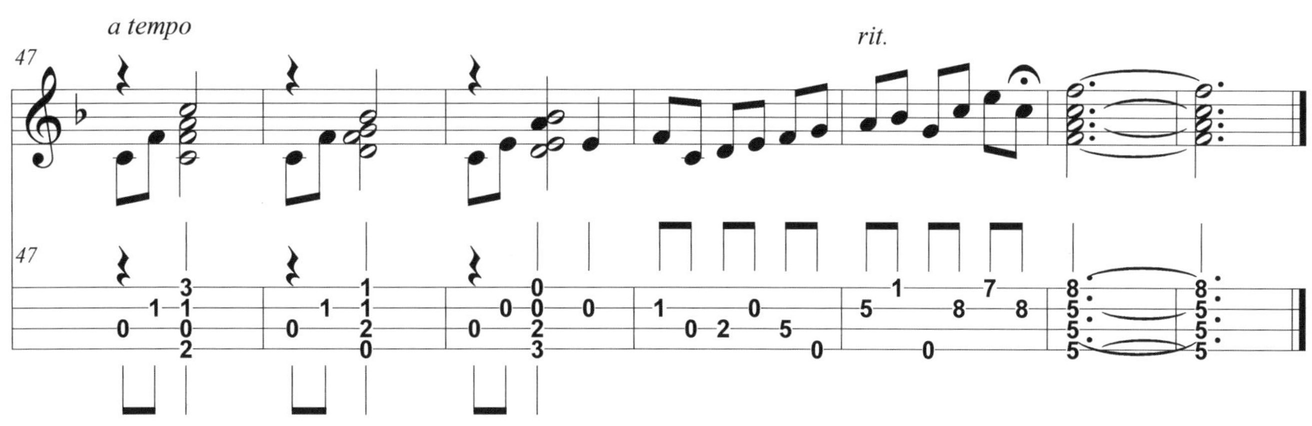
a tempo
rit.

Johnny Has Gone for a Soldier

Civil War Ballad

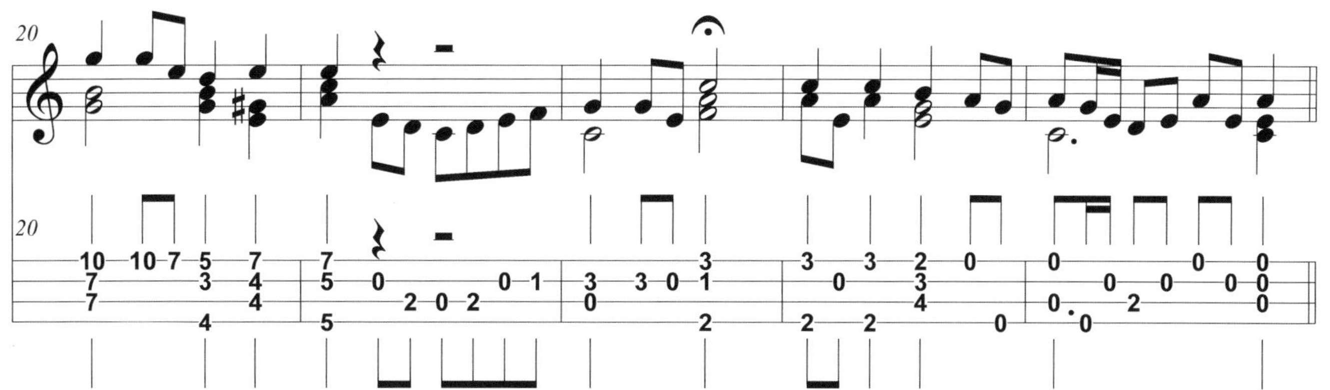
20
20

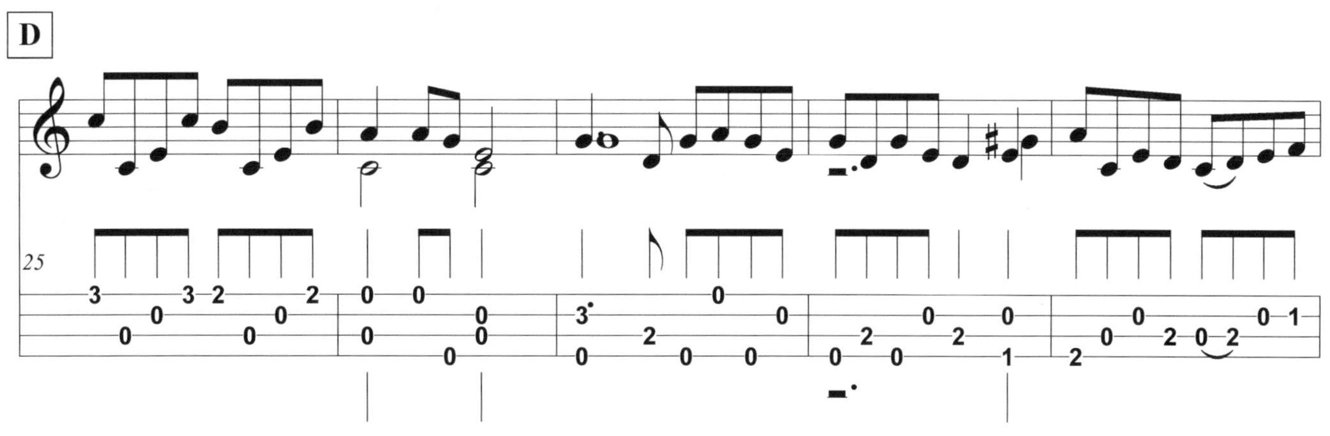
D
25

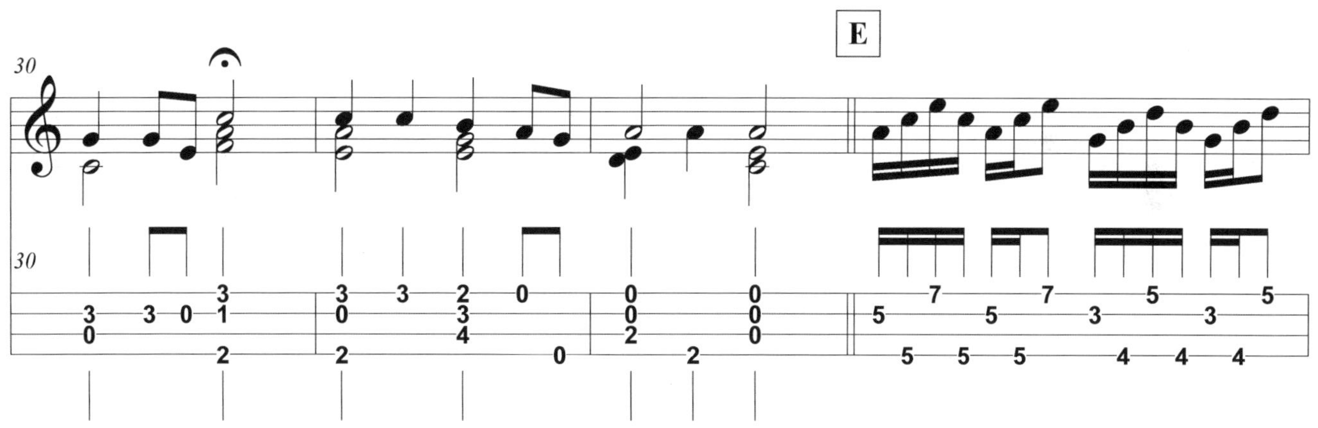
30
E
30

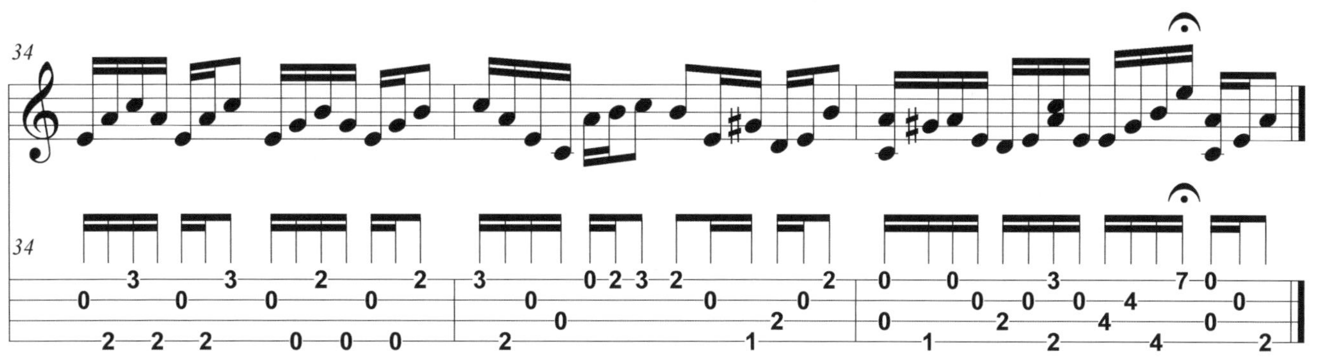
34
34

Lorena

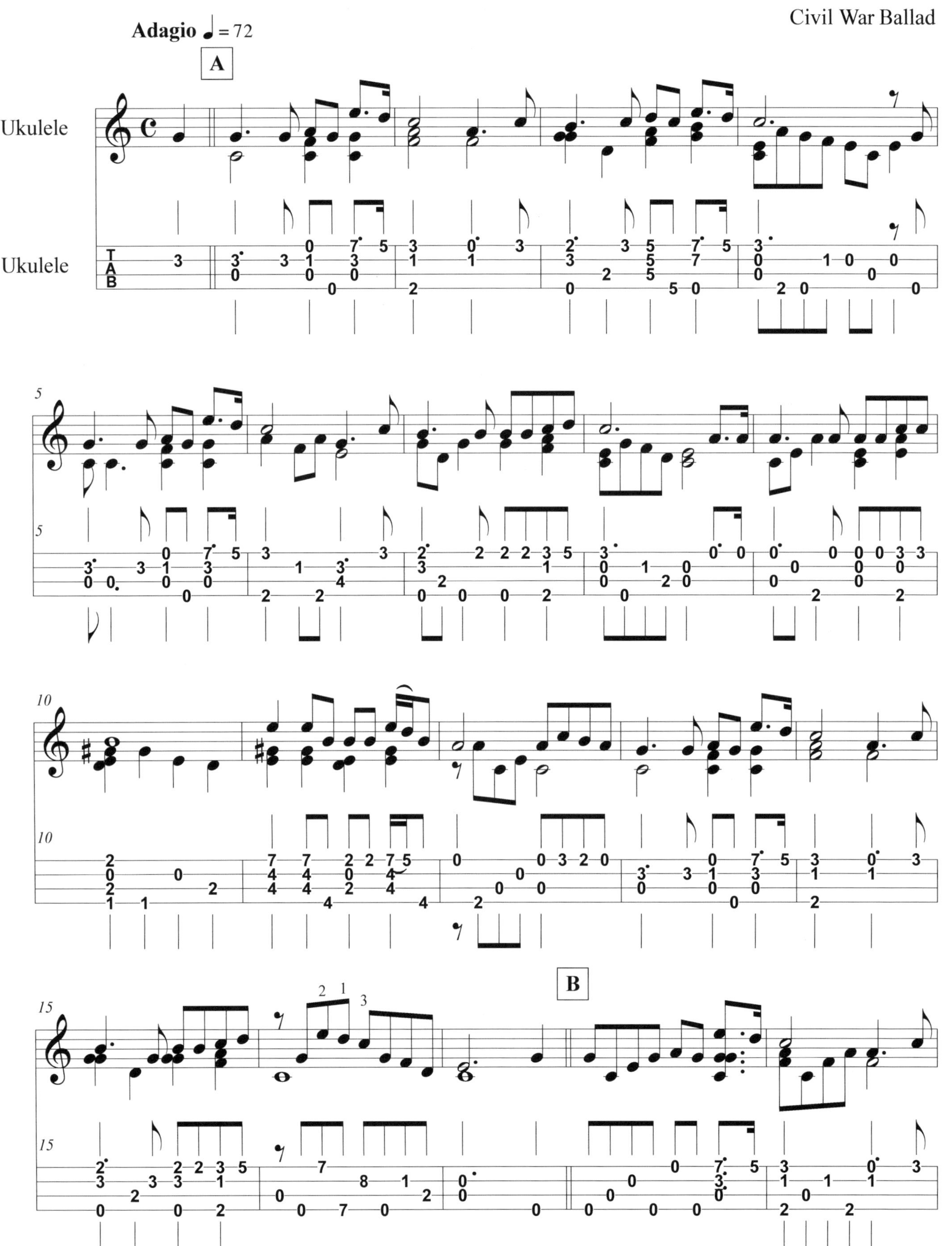

a tempo
rit.

Black Sunday

Andante ♩ = 84 — Oklahoma, April 14, 1935 — William Bay

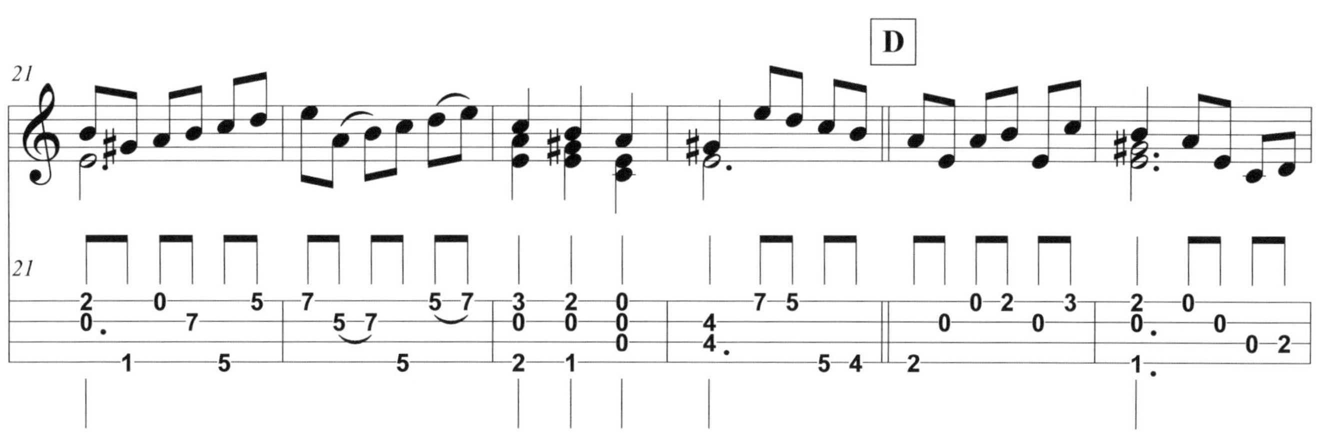
21
D
21

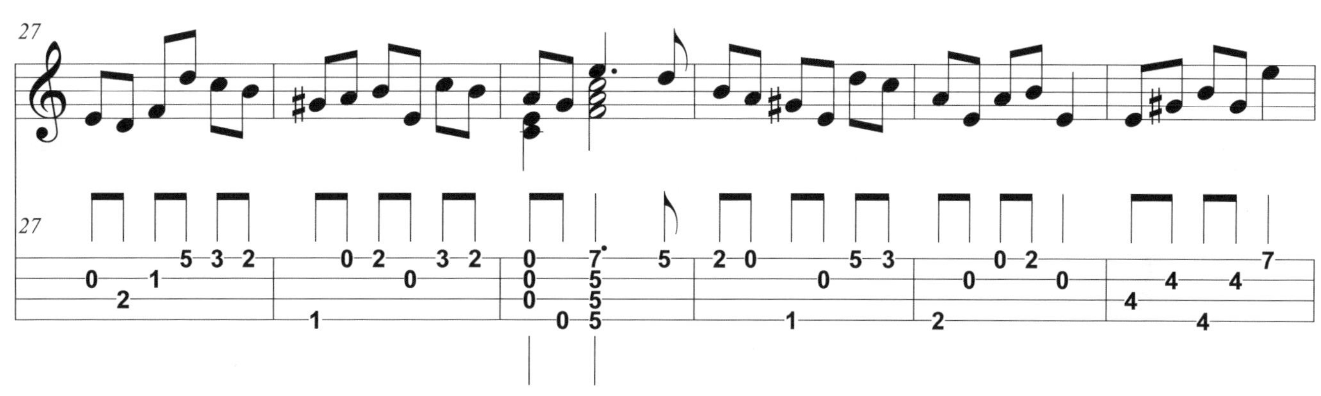
27
27

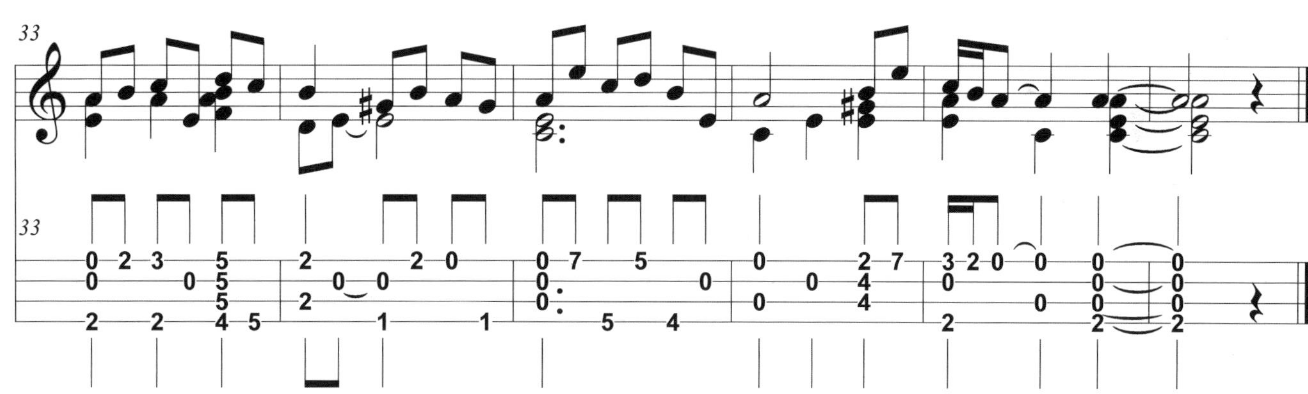
33
33

Prairie Sunset

William Bay

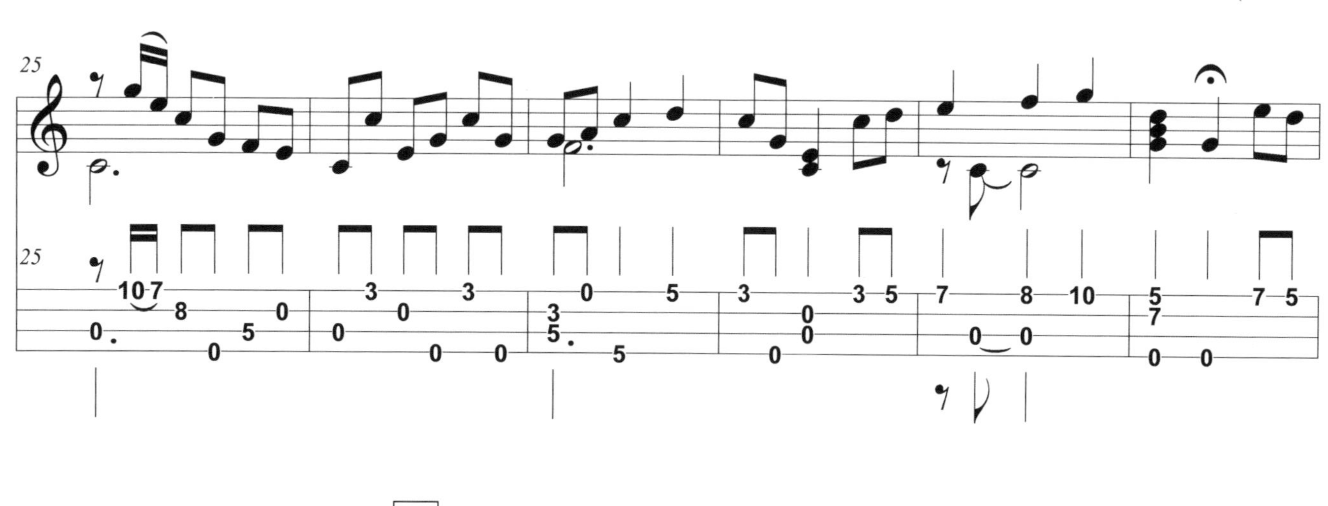

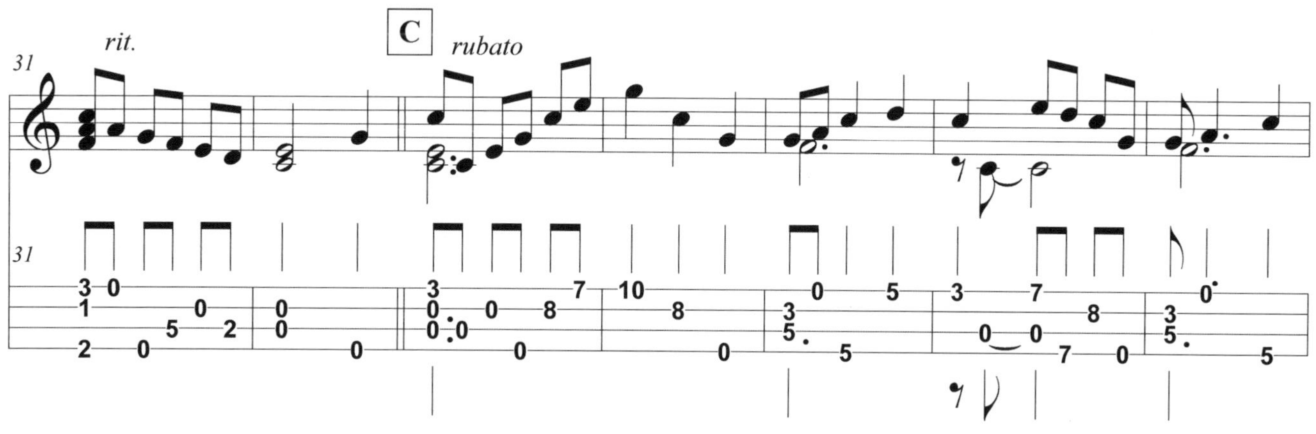
rit.
C
rubato

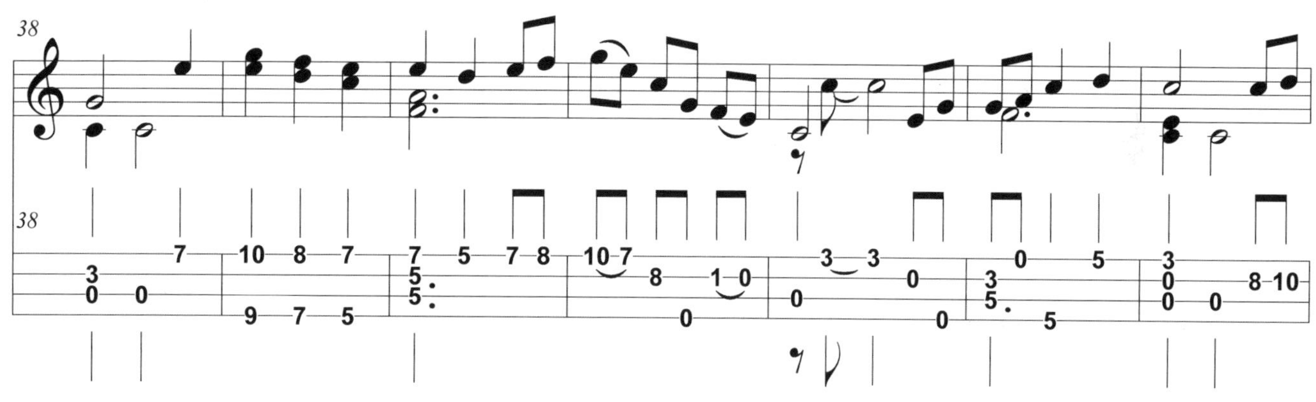

Shady Grove

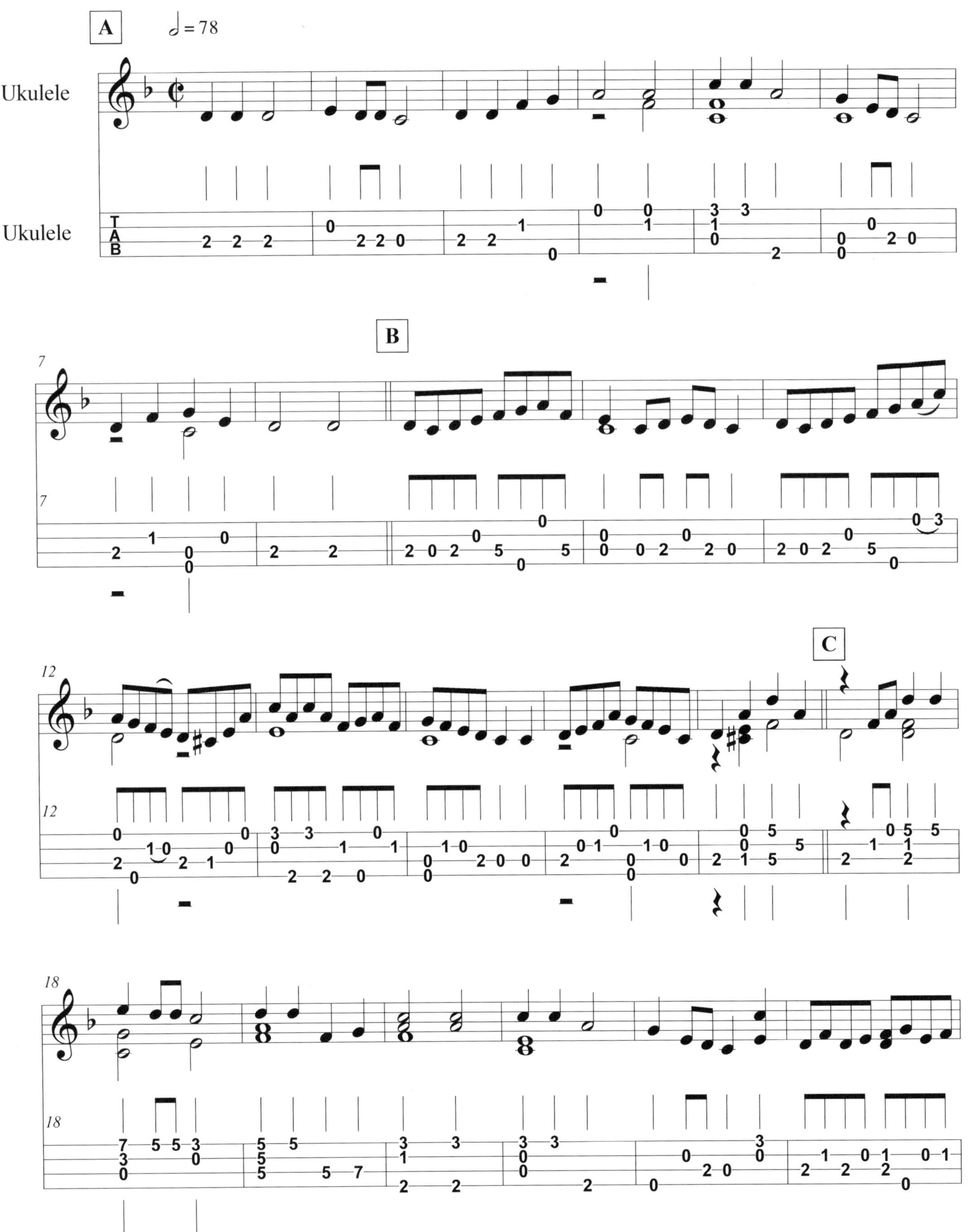

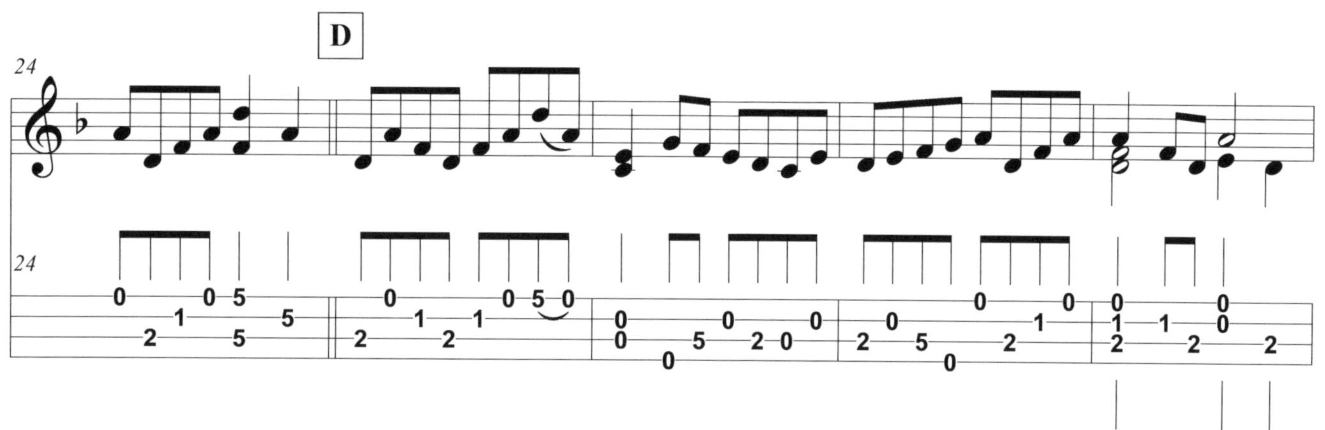
D
24

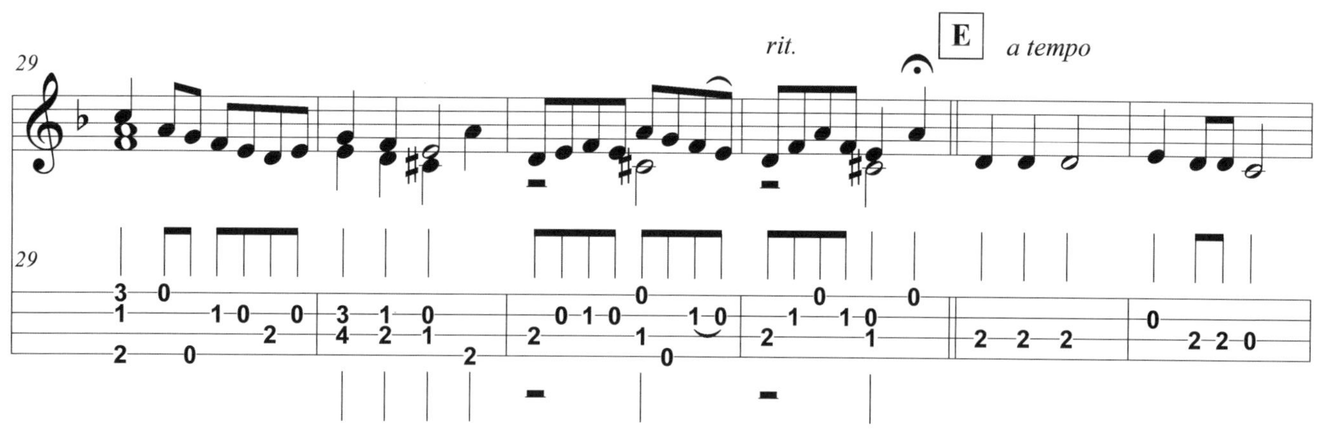
rit.
E
a tempo
29

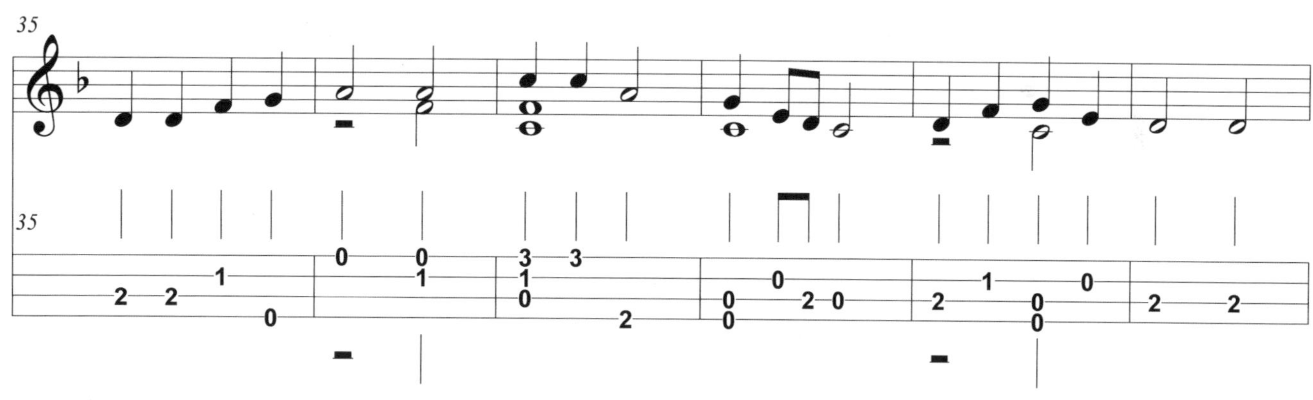
35

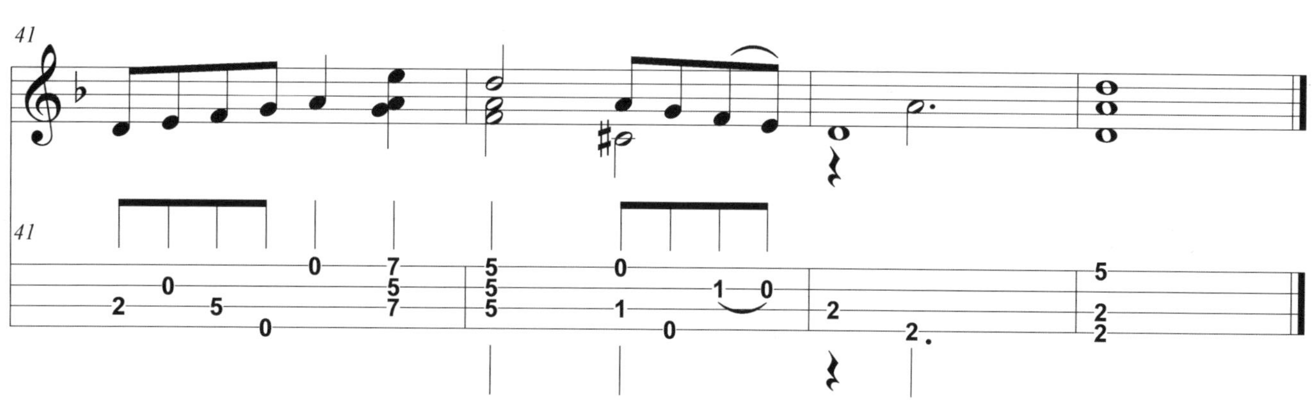
41

Shenandoah

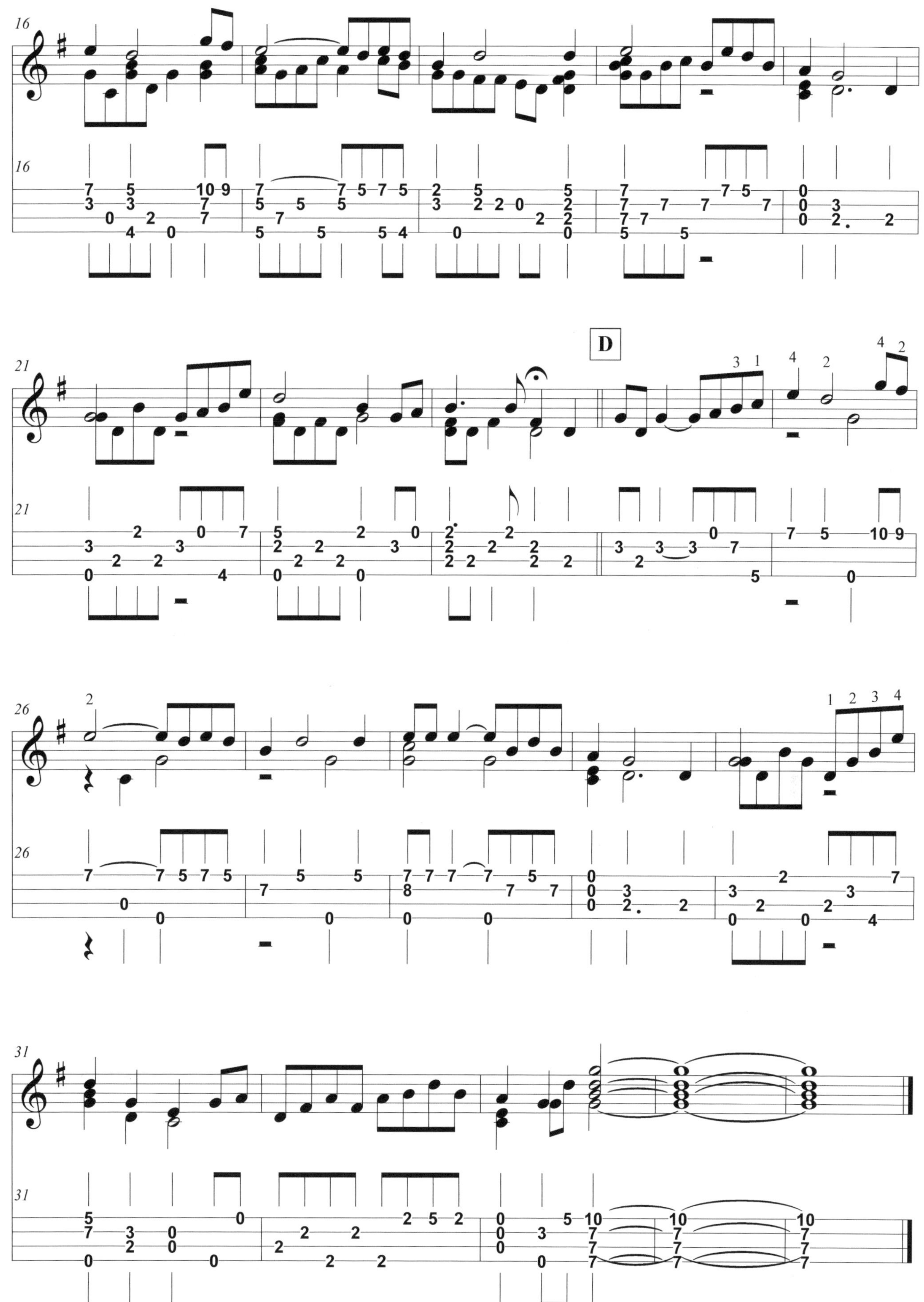
D

The Lonesome Dove

D
rit.
E
a tempo

Trail of Tears

William Bay

D

I Dream of Jeanie with the Light Brown Hair

17
21
C
25
29
rit.

Just A-Wearyin' for You

Carrie Jacobs Bond

C

Mighty Lak' a Rose

Ethelbert Nevin
(1862-1901)

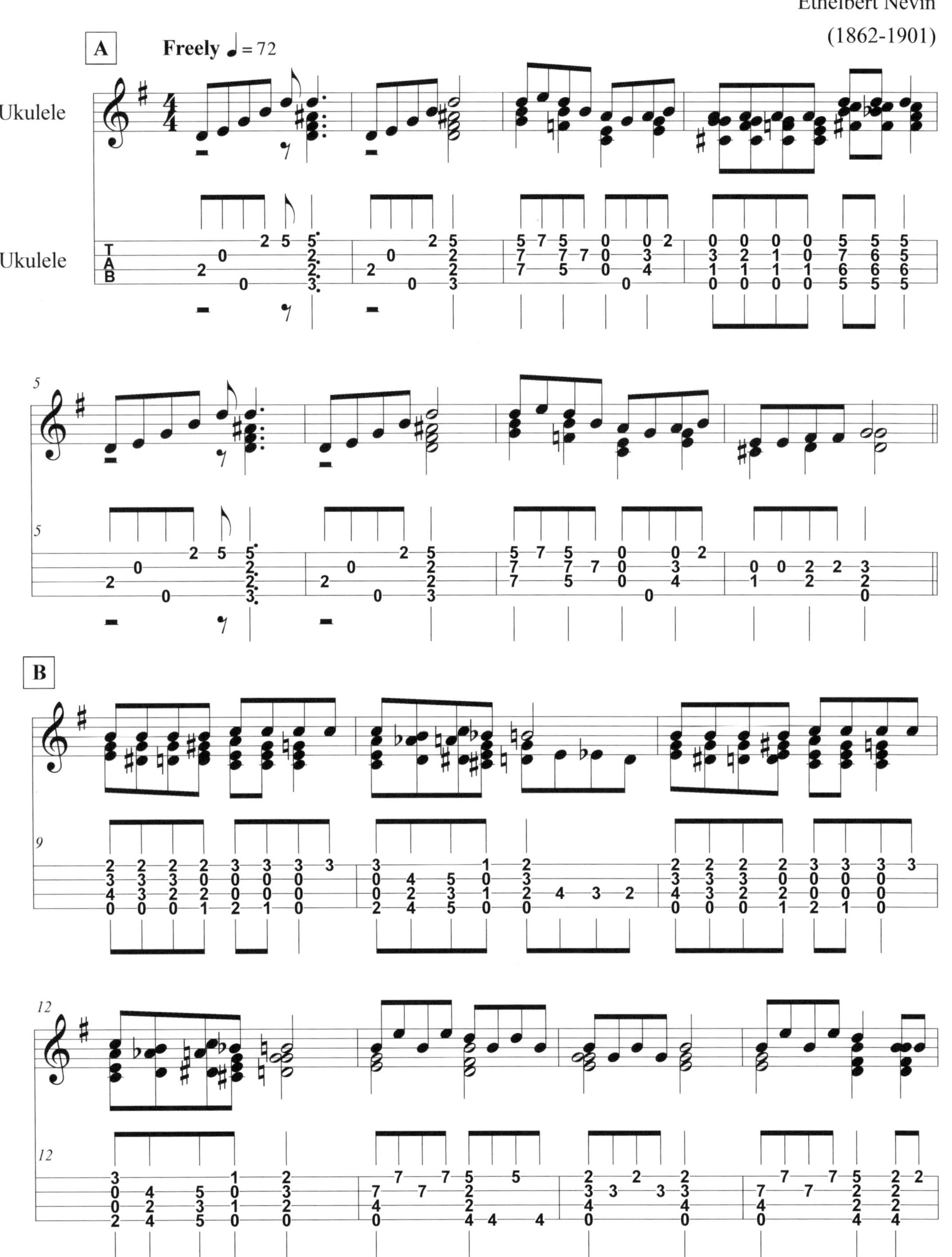

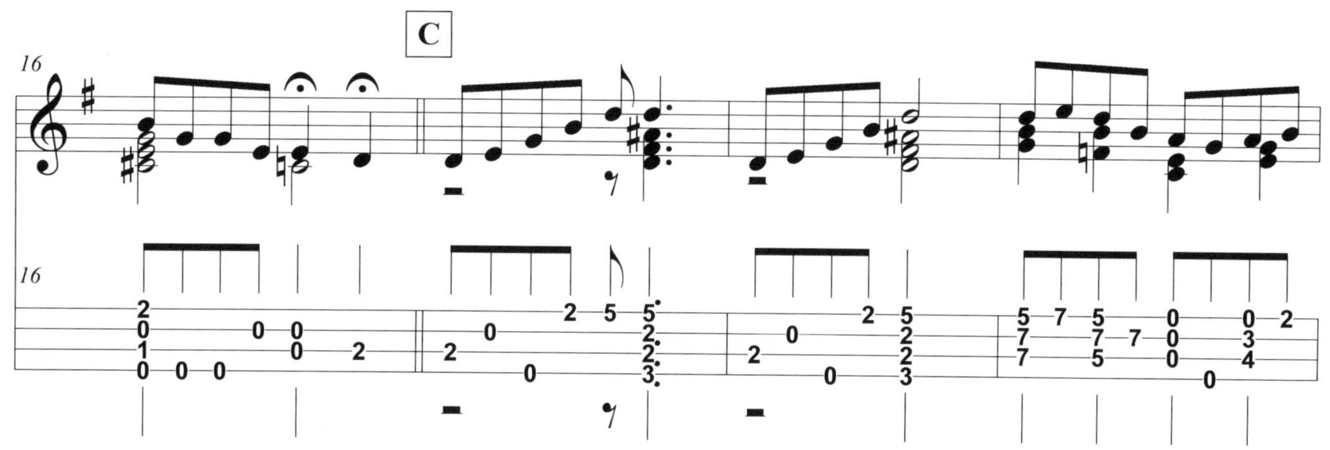
C

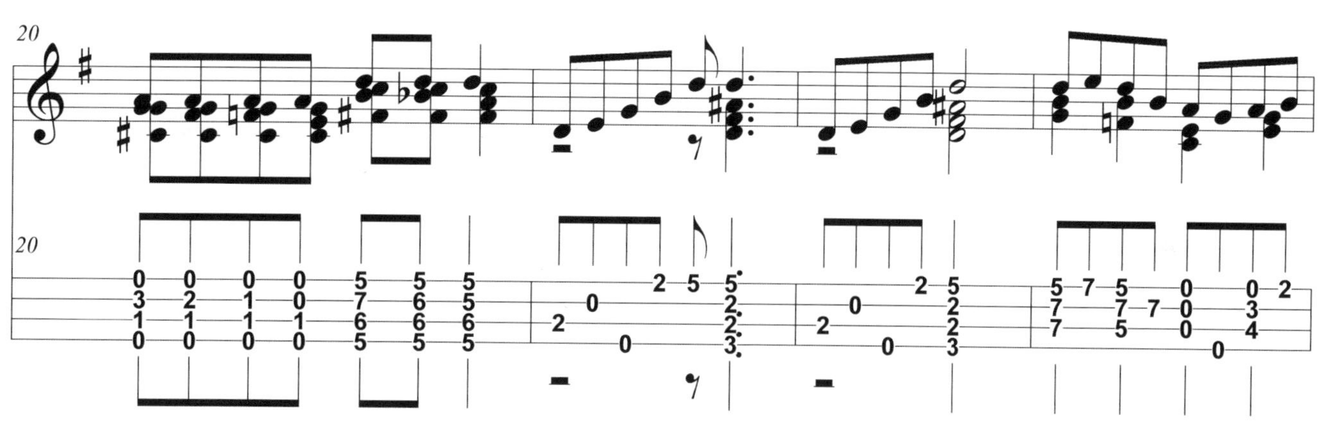

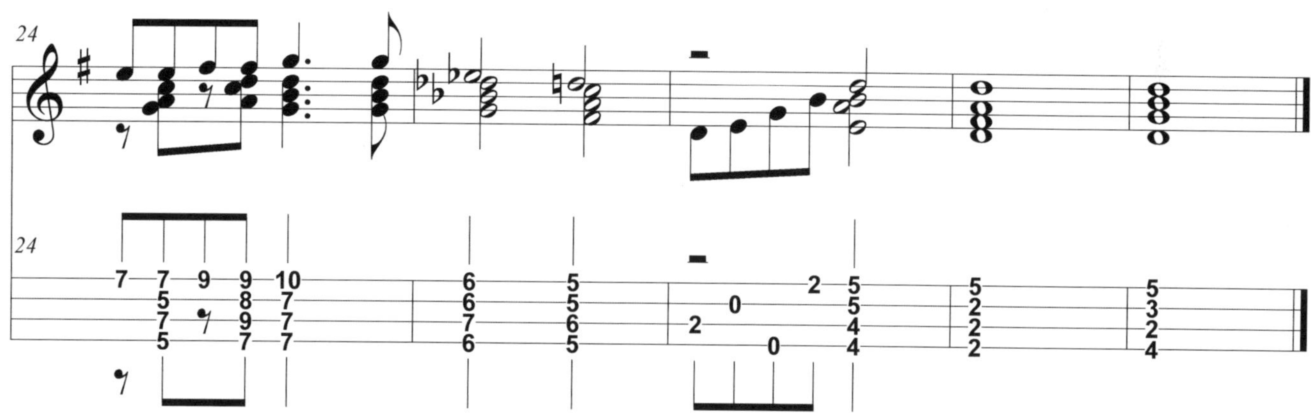

To a Wild Rose

Edward MacDowell

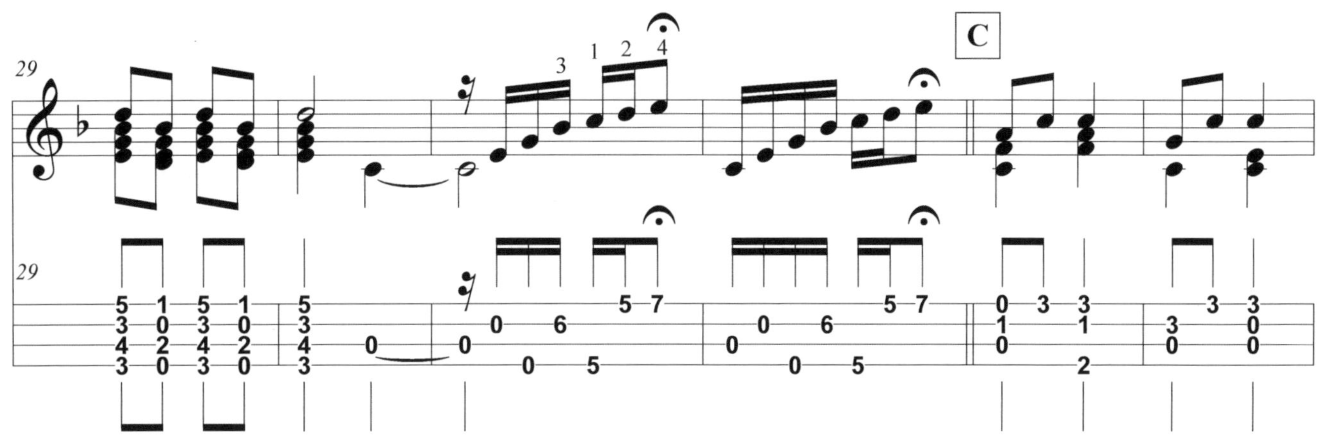
29
C

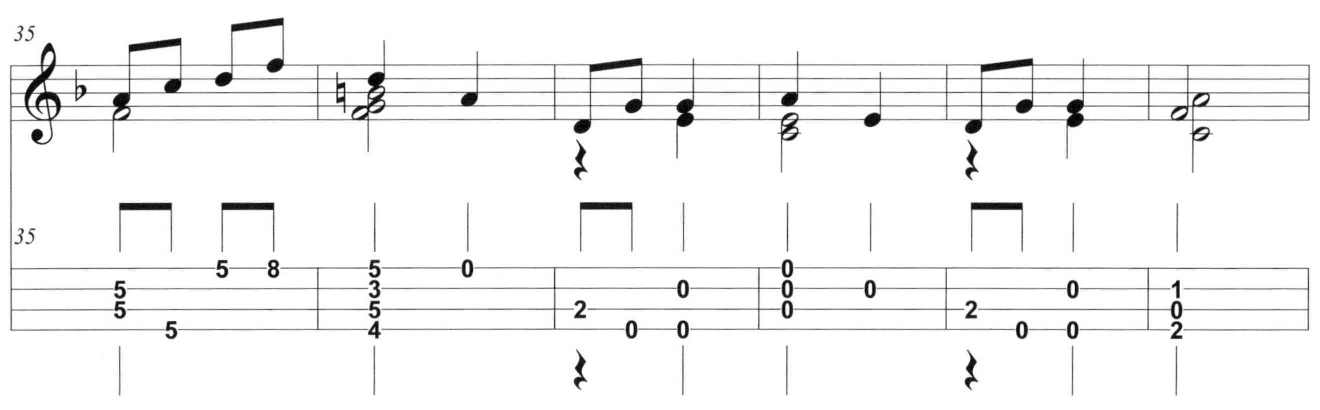
35

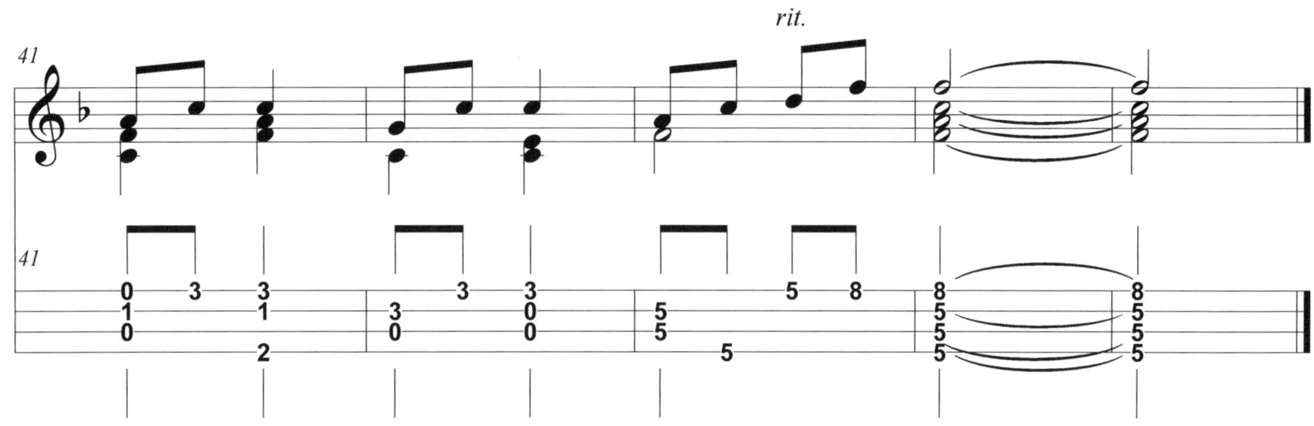
41
rit.

Beautiful Dreamer

Stephen Foster

rit.

Pretty Peggy - O

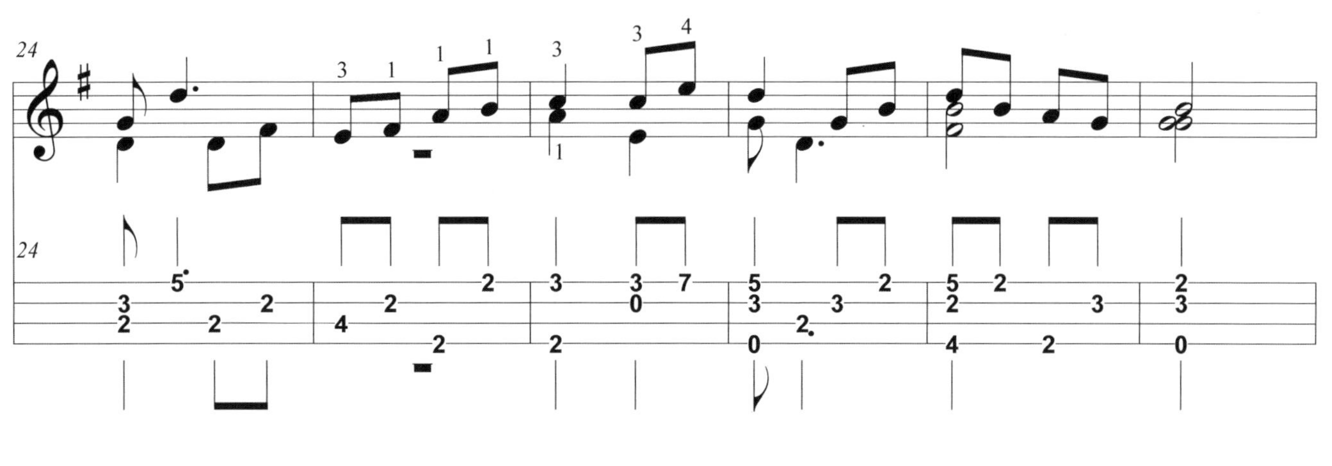
24
3 1 1 1 3 3 4
1
24
5
3 2
2 2
4 2 2
2
3 3 7
0
2
5 2
3 3
0 2
5 2
2 3
4 2
2
3
0

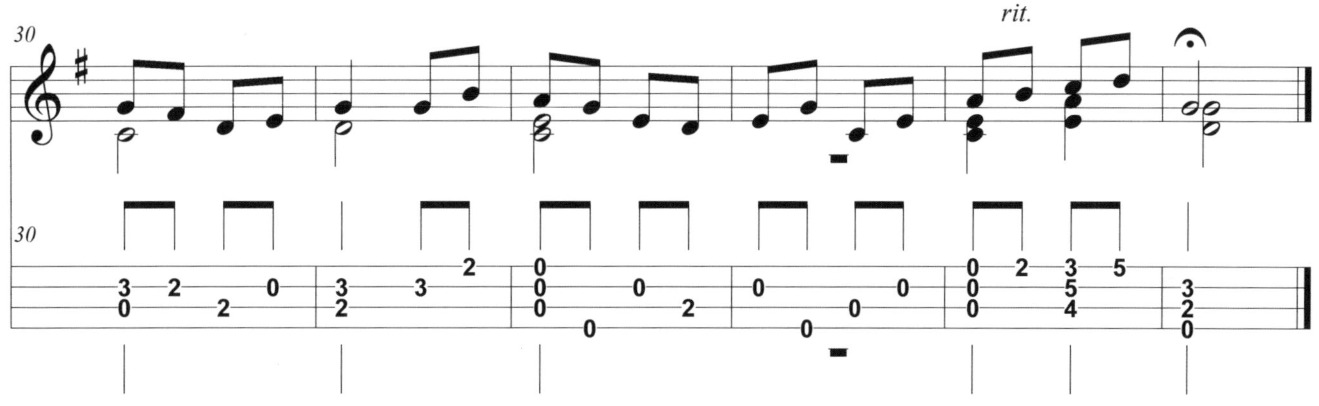
30
rit.
30
3 2 0
0 2
3 3 2
2
0 0
0
0 2
0
0 0
0 0
0 2 3 5
0 5
0 4
3
2
0

Hard Times Come Again No More

About the Author

Born in 1979, Ondřej Šárek earned a master's degree in Composition at The Janacek Academy of Music and Performing Arts while simultaneously studying Musicology at The Faculty of Arts at Masaryk University in Brno in the Czech Republic. An award-winning participant in several composition competitions, his chamber orchestra, symphonic and choral works are performed internationally. He has also written three mini-operas plus music for film, television, and theater productions.

As a skillful multi-instrumentalist, he devotes his time to playing and composing for piano, guitar, banjo, ukulele, Irish bouzouki, concertina, diatonic accordion, and mandola. He has arranged solo collections for various instruments, many of which have been released by Mel Bay Publications. Ondřej is also one of the leading arrangers of music for the ukulele, an instrument he hopes will regain its former prominence.

Other Mel Bay Ukulele Books

Lively Ukulele Tunes (Šárek)
Ukulele Picking Tunes - Fun Songs to Play (Šárek)
Ukulele Picking Tunes - Early Music Gems (Šárek)
Children's Ukulele Method (Andrews)
Dirt Simple Uke (Carr)
Easy Ukulele Method in Notes and Tab Book 1 (Dempler)
Easy Ukulele Method in Notes and Tab Book 2 (Dempler)
First Lessons Fingerstyle Ukulele (Gilewitz)
Fun with the Ukulele (M. Bay)
Fun with Strums: Ukulele (W. Bay)
Learn to Play Fingerstyle Solos for Ukulele (Nelson)
Learn to Play Slack Key Ukulele (Nelson)
Modern Ukulele Method (Carr)
Open Tunings for Ukulele (Šárek)
Ukulele for Seniors (Carr)
Ukulele Method in D Tuning (Roy Smeck)
You Can Teach Yourself Uke (W. Bay)
Children's Ukulele Chord Book (Andrews)
Left-Handed Uke Chord Chart (W. Bay)
Left-Handed Uke Chords (M. Bay)
Mastering Chord Inversions for Ukulele (Nelson)
Uke Chord Chart (W. Bay)
Ukulele Chords (M. Bay)
Uke Chords Made Easy (W. Bay)
Uke Rhythms: Picking and Strumming Patterns (Driscoll)
Understanding Ukulele Chords (van Renesse)
20 Caribbean Pieces for Ukulele (Carr)
20 Celtic Fingerstyle Uke Tunes (MacKillop)
20 Easy Classical Uke Pieces for Kids (MacKillop)
20 Old-Time American Tunes Arranged for Ukulele (MacKillop)
20 Popular Uke Tunes for Kids (MacKillop)
20 Spanish Baroque Pieces by Gaspar Sanz Arranged for Uke (MacKillop)
Children's Songs for Solo Ukulele (Carr)
Classics for Ukulele (Šárek)
Famous Solos and Duets for the Ukulele (King)
Favorite Classical Themes for Ukulele (Coe)
Favorite Fingerstyle Solos for Ukulele (Nelson)
Favorite Old-Time American Songs for Ukulele (Nelson)
Fingerstyle Duets for Ukulele (Nelson)
First Jams: Ukulele (Andrews)
Folk Songs for Solo Ukulele (Carr)
Francisco Tárrega for Ukulele (Šárek)
Gospel Favorites for solo Ukulele (Carr)
Great Melodies for Solo Ukulele (Carr)